Understanding Families:
Children's Perspectives

ON ꓘOLLEGE

Virginia Morrow

D

D1421965

SUPPORTED BY

JR
JOSEPH
ROWNTREE
FOUNDATION

NATIONAL CHILDREN'S BUREAU

**NATIONAL
CHILDREN'S
BUREAU**

The National Children's Bureau (NCB) works to identify and promote the well-being and interests of all children and young people across every aspect of their lives.

It encourages professionals and policy makers to see the needs of the whole child and emphasises the importance of multidisciplinary, cross-agency partnerships. The NCB has adopted and works within the UN Convention on the Rights of the Child.

It collects and disseminates information about children and promotes good practice in children's services through research, policy and practice development, membership, publications, conferences, training and an extensive library and information service.

Several Councils and Fora are based at the NCB and contribute significantly to the breadth of its influence. It also works in partnership with Children in Scotland and Children in Wales and other voluntary organisations concerned for children and their families.

The **Joseph Rowntree Foundation** has supported this project as part of its programme of research and innovative development projects, which it hopes will be of value to policy makers and practitioners.

The views expressed in this book are those of the author and not necessarily those of the National Children's Bureau or the Joseph Rowntree Foundation.

ISBN 1 900990 27 X

Published by National Children's Bureau Enterprises Ltd, 8 Wakley Street, London EC1V 7QE

National Children's Bureau Enterprises Ltd is the trading company for the National Children's Bureau (Registered Charity number 258825).

Typeset by LaserScript Ltd, Mitcham, Surrey CR4 4NA

Printed and bound in the United Kingdom by Redwood Books, Trowbridge BA14 8RN

Contents

Acknowledgements

The author would like to offer her gratitude to the children and the schools who participated in this research, without whose cooperation the project would not have been possible. Thanks too to Georgia and Hannah, who helped pilot the questions.

She is also thankful for the research assistance of Julie Jessop, who helped with the data analysis and final writing up of the project, also Jill Brown and Sally Roberts at the Centre for Family Research, University of Cambridge, for their help; and Dasia Black Gutman, Gill Dunne, and especially Gill Jones and Kurshida Mirza, for their insightful comments on earlier drafts. The author is grateful to Professor Martin Richards, joint grant-holder, and to Barbara Ballard and Susan Taylor for their input during the course of the project. The author would also like to acknowledge the assistance afforded by the Advisory Group.

ADVISORY GROUP
Erica De'ath, NCVCCO, London
Gerison Lansdown, Children's Rights Development Unit, London
Sophie Laws and Bridget Pettit, Save the Children Fund
Professor Margaret O'Brien, University of North London
Dr Alan Prout, Keele University
Professor Martin Richards, Centre for Family Research, University of Cambridge
Dr Helen Roberts, Barnardos
Dr Marjorie Smith, Thomas Coram Research Unit, University of London
Susan Taylor, Joseph Rowntree Foundation
Lennox Thomas, NAFSIYAT

Summary and Findings

Summary

Family forms are changing rapidly and children are increasingly likely to have some experience of living in family types other than the so-called 'traditional nuclear norm' of two parent-two child. At the same time the UK is a multicultural society and contains a diversity of family patterns and cultural traditions. However, the image of 'the family' as nuclear remains pervasive. Further, recent changes in social policy such as the UN Convention on the Rights of the Child and the Children Act 1989 have highlighted the need to listen to 'the child's voice' when decisions are being made about their care and welfare. This report describes a qualitative study which explores how children define and reflect upon the concept of 'family'. It provides background information about how children conceptualise 'family' which will be useful to practitioners attempting to incorporate children's views into practice.

The study had two main aims:

- to describe how children perceive and define the concept 'family'
- to provide insight into ways of 'listening to children'.

The research explored the following questions:

1. To what extent do children's views conform to stereotypical images of the typical family?
2. What are the important defining characteristics of 'a family'?
3. Who is important to children?
4. Do children themselves feel 'listened to' and do children want to be involved in decisions concerning them?
5. In relation to these questions, are there differences related to age, gender, ethnic background and location?

The research is based on empirical data gathered from 183 children aged between eight and 14 in schools in two parts of East Anglia, a rural area and a large town with a population which included British Muslims originating from Mirpur and Azad Kashmir in Pakistan.

Findings

1. Overall, children appeared to have an accepting, inclusive view of what counts as family and their definitions did not centre around biological relatedness or the 'nuclear' norm. The research shows that children can be constructive, reflective commentators. It shows that children have a realistic view of family life, and are aware of a wide variation in family practices and structures.

2. When children defined in their own words what a family is and what families are for, it emerged that love, care, mutual respect and support were the key characteristics of 'family'. This was the case regardless of gender, ethnic background, and location.

   Children's definitions were more complex the older they were. When children were asked about their beliefs as to what counted as 'family', younger children were more likely than older children to see children, marriage and physical presence as being the key components of 'a family'. Older children were more likely to see the nature or quality of the relationships between family members as being the key defining characteristic of whether or not a particular configuration constitutes a family.

3. Who is important to children? The centrality to children of parents, especially **mothers**, as providers of physical and emotional care, was clear from the children's accounts. Gender roles between parents are also clearly differentiated. Girls in particular described their mothers as important as someone to talk to.

   Sibling relationships were also meaningful. While such relationships are rarely conflict-free, they are often underpinned by a good deal of mutual affection, and in some cases siblings clearly provide a good deal of support to each other. Some children of Pakistani origin described large nuclear families and described a pattern of playing with siblings, rather than friends, in a way that was different to other children in the study.

The social life of some children appeared to revolve around their **relatives and extended kin**. Contrary to stereotypical assumptions, children of Pakistani origin did not describe extended families any more or less than other children.

Friendships were important to the older children in the sample. Girls in particular described their close friends as crucial for emotional support, though this was the case for some boys too.

4. Do children feel listened to? In response to questions exploring 'being listened to', children in the study were asking to be able to 'have a say' in what happens to them, rather than to make decisions *per se*. There is an important distinction to be drawn between being asked to make a decision and feeling that one is being provided with information, consulted and listened to. Some children did feel they are listened to within their families, others did not, and others showed a sophisticated awareness that 'decision making' may be problematic.

5. There were some differences related to age, gender, and ethnic background. Younger children presented fairly concrete explanations, describing the way their families provide for them. Older children drew on abstract concepts of the quality of relationships. The responses of the children of Pakistani origin need to be seen in the context of their cultural and religious traditions, in which a strong sense of mutual family obligations is clearly expressed, and in which divorce may be unusual. On the whole, though, the people who were important to children, regardless of ethnic background, were the people who are available to them, and their households provided a supportive setting.

1. Introduction and methods

Background

This research is set in the context of two sets of recent social changes. Firstly, contemporary children are likely to experience a variety of family settings as they pass through childhood. Recent statistics show that 38 per cent of children (under 16 or 16 to 18 in full time education and living in the household) live in average 'nuclear family' households (that is, two parents and two children); 20 per cent live with a lone parent and one in 12 children live in stepfamilies (CSO, 1994). At the same time, as many writers have pointed out, images of 'the family' as nuclear are all-pervasive and ethnocentric (Bernardes, 1997; Ennew, 1994; Gubrium and Holstein, 1990; Holland, 1992; Makrinioti, 1994; Morgan, 1996). The UK is a multicultural society and consists of a diversity of family patterns and cultural traditions, and norms of kinship and family obligations may differ between and among minority ethnic groups (Robertson Elliot, 1996; Ahmad, 1996).

Secondly, changes in social policy have prioritised the need to 'listen to children' and 'attend to the child's voice' (see Lansdown, 1994, 1995; Roberts and Sachdev, 1996). The Children Act 1989 stipulates that courts shall have particular regard to 'the ascertainable wishes and feelings of the child concerned (considered in the light of his [sic] age and under-standing)' (Section 1(3)(a)). The UN Convention on the Rights of the Child provides a framework for addressing rights relating not only to children's need for care, protection and adequate provision, but also for participation (Lansdown, 1994, 1995):

> States Parties shall assure to the child who is capable of forming his or her own views the right to express those views freely in all

matters affecting the child, the views of the child being given due
weight in accordance with the age and maturity of the child . . .
For this purpose, the child shall, in particular, be provided with
the opportunity to be heard in any judicial and administrative
procedures affecting the child. (Article 12, UN Convention on the
Rights of the Child)

However, there is remarkably little research into how
children make sense of contemporary patterns of family life,
and children's notions of family in general have remained
relatively unexplored by social researchers (O'Brien, Alldred
and Jones, 1996; Hill and Tisdall, 1997). Most knowledge of
children's experiences of their families comes from adults,
from parents, from professionals such as social workers,
lawyers or psychologists, or from adult recollections of their
own difficult childhood experiences (see for example Mitchell,
1985; Walczak and Burns, 1984). Few studies have attempted
to explore children's definitions and ideas about family in any
systematic way. Exceptions are a recent study with 8 to 9 year
olds in East London, which found that children have complex
and often contradictory conceptualisations of 'family'
(O'Brien, Alldred and Jones, 1996; O'Brien and Jones,
1996), and a small-scale study exploring children's accounts
of family in a range of family settings (Moore, Sixsmith and
Knowles, 1996), which challenges dominant ideas about the
effect of families on children and shows that children's
perspectives on what is important may differ from those of
adults/parents' perspectives (see also Clarke, Craig and
Glendinning, 1996 on children's views of child support; Butler
and Williamson, 1994).

Aims of the research

This report explores how children define and reflect upon the
concept of 'family'. Given the changing nature of family
structures, and given the emphasis on the need to listen to
'the child's voice' when decisions are being made about their
care and welfare, what are the defining characteristics of 'a
family', from children's perspectives? Who is important to
them? And, since 'children' are not a homogenous group, how
does this change with age, and are there differences related to
gender, ethnic background and location? Further, given that
the research is about 'listening to children', do children
themselves feel 'listened to'? To what extent do they want to

be involved in making decisions that will affect their lives, and how do they like to express themselves?

Research setting and sample

Research was carried out in 1996 and 1997 with eight mixed-ability class-groups of children in four schools in East Anglia, two village schools (one Secondary, and a feeder Church of England junior school); and two town schools (a Secondary school and a feeder junior school).

In the Village junior school, the classes were arranged in mixed Year 3/4 (8–9 year olds) and mixed Year 5/6 (10–11 year olds) and research was carried out with one class of each. In the Village secondary school, research was undertaken with one tutor group of Year 8 (12 year olds) and one of Year 9 (13 year olds); children came from a wide catchment area, but this is not a remote rural area and there are several large towns nearby. Children were from a range of socio-economic backgrounds, and there were no children from minority ethnic backgrounds in the Village sample.

The Town schools were located in a large town in East Anglia with a significant inner city population of British Muslims originating from Mirpur and Azad Kashmir in Pakistan. The junior school has a high proportion of children of Pakistani origin. I worked with one class of Year 3 (8 year old) children and one class of Year 5 (10 year old) children. The children are bilingual (or trilingual) and English is not their first language. There is no secondary school in the centre of the town where families of Pakistani origin live, so research was carried out in one of the outlying secondary schools. The proportion of children from a minority ethnic background in the school is about 20 per cent and includes African-Caribbean and other South Asian, so the numbers of children of Pakistani origin in the sample are small. Research was carried out with one group of Year 8 and one group of Year 9 children. The school was built in an area of public and private housing, free schools meals rates are the highest in the county (only households on Income Support or Job Seekers Allowance are entitled to free school meals).

The reasons for carrying out research with these samples of children were as follows. Firstly, the research aimed to explore stereotypical assumptions about kinship and family with a minority ethnic group assumed to be very different from the majority culture. About 75 per cent of people of Pakistani origin in the town in which research was carried out originate from the Mirpur area in Pakistan (the historical reasons for these migration patterns are described by Saifullah Khan, 1979, and Shaw, 1988). As Hylton notes, Pakistanis are a well-established minority ethnic group in the UK. The children in the study were mostly, but not all, third-generation immigrants, but the notion of 'generation' may be misleading because many of the children described how they (or other family members) return to Pakistan for visits and the links they have with Pakistan are clearly very important. Research with adults confirms this: Modood, Beishon and Virdee (1994) in a qualitative study of ethnic identity among different minority ethnic groups in the UK noted that Pakistanis had a good deal of contact with family in Pakistan. Traditionally, Pakistani kinship patterns are based on extended family groups and wider 'clan' (biraderi) networks, and children's ideas about the concept of family need to be seen in this context. Hylton suggests:

> group cohesion and links with family networks are very strong, resulting in a strong aversion and stigma to divorce, and restrictions on remarriage. Marriage is usually sanctioned within the biraderi network . . . The biraderi network, which could encompass hundreds of people who share the same family name, is a wider unit than the extended family. Generally divorce is not encouraged, but remarriage is easier for both women and men if they marry another divorcee. (Hylton, 1995, p. 15)

Family and kinship structures are further complicated by 'strong Islamic principles contained in the Qur'ān which emphasise the importance of family obligations and inter-dependence (Hylton, 1995, p. 15; see also Afshar, 1995; Saifullah Khan, 1979; Shaw, 1988).

Secondly, all children in the UK are subject to the same laws, social policies and practitioner-input regardless of ethnic background, and these laws and social policies may in themselves be ethnocentric and discriminatory.

Thirdly, the research aimed to redress an imbalance in that the experiences and perspectives of children from minority ethnic groups are under-represented in social research in general. Finally, the samples were selected to reflect age and gender differences, and schools were chosen to reflect a range of socio-economic circumstances. The sample distribution across these variables is shown in Table 1.1.

Table 1.1   **Age and gender distribution of sample (children of Pakistani origin in bold)**

Age	Village, boys	Village, girls	Town, boys	Town, girls
8	8	10	7	6
9	5	8	1	1
10	5	2	9	1 + 13
11	7	10	2	2
12	11	10	2 + 1	2
13	7	13	3 + 4	9
14	2	1	10 + 5	5 + 1
Totals	45	54	15 + 29	17 + 23

Perspectives and research techniques

The perspective taken in research has implications for how data are collected and interpreted. The approach taken in this project follows the model developed by James and Prout (1990), who suggest that 'children's social relationships and cultures are worthy of study in their own right, independent of the perspectives and concerns of adults' (p. 8). This envisages children as research subjects comparable with adults, as competent co-producers of data, but with different (rather than lesser) competencies (see James, 1995). This has implications for the methods used in studying children: children have different abilities, and can be skilled and confident in different media of communication (drawings, written work, stories), which researchers can usefully draw upon.

The project thus used multiple research strategies (see Brannen, 1992; Lucchini, 1996) to explore the issues raised by the research questions, building up a picture of how children perceive and define 'family'. The intention was not to focus on *individual* personal experiences and family backgrounds. Rather, the research aimed to explore norms, beliefs, and representations, and children's ideas and use of language about the concept of 'family'. Qualitative techniques were used:

- structured activities
  - draw-and-write on 'who is important to me?'
  - sentence completion on 'what is a family?' and 'what are families for?'

- a short questionnaire asking whether or not five one-sentence descriptions of family type (vignettes) counted as family
- open-ended group discussions exploring
  - children's responses to the questionnaire
  - what they read, watched on TV, and media images of families
  - children's involvement in decision making and the extent to which they felt listened to, in their families, schools and the wider community.

Discussions were taped and transcribed. All data were coded and sorted using the qualitative data analysis package ATLAS/ti. The advantages and disadvantages of the data collection techniques, ethical questions raised in conducting research with children on a sensitive topic, issues of informed consent, and ethnicity, are explored in more detail in Morrow and Richards (1996), Morrow (1997, 1998, forthcoming); see also Alderson (1995). As noted, the project aimed to explore stereotypical assumptions about kinship and family with minority ethnic groups. The same research methods were used by the same researcher for all children (in other words, if a Mirpuri facilitator had carried out the research using the children's mother-tongue, a different picture might have emerged). Thus, the names in the sentences were not changed for the children of Pakistani origin, and given that the situations described relate to white European situations, the children may well be reflecting normative views of UK cultural stereotypes. However, one of the aims of the research was to explore how pervasive these stereotypes are.

Structure of the report

The remainder of the report describes the main findings. Section 2 discusses what children counted as family, and analyses children's responses to the yes/no questions of the vignettes and then explores their discussions of these questions. Section 3 describes how they defined family and the functions of family and focuses on their accounts of parents. Section 4 discusses their accounts of siblings, kin, friends and others. Section 5 explores children's discussions of 'being listened to' and having a say in decisions. The final section discusses the conclusions and implications of the research. For the purposes of analysis, I have divided the children into 'younger' (primary) and 'older' (secondary), and where there were differences according to ethnic background, age, gender, and location, I have explored these in detail. The children chose their own pseudonyms and these have been used in the report.

2. What counts as 'family'?

This section explores children's beliefs about what counts as family. Previous research has explored how children conceptualise 'family' by asking them to state whether they thought a particular household configuration counts as family (O'Brien, Alldred and Jones, 1996; Gilby and Pederson, 1982 for Canada), and in doing so found that younger children in particular reflect quite traditional views. This exercise was repeated in the current project, and this section explores children's responses to and discussions of five one-sentence 'stories' which describe various family configurations, including a childless couple, cohabiting, divorced, and lone father households. These hypothetical situations (vignettes) provided a way of exploring children's beliefs and norms about what counts as a family (see also Finch and Mason, 1993 with adults). The questions were:

1. *John and Susan are a married couple without any children. Are they a family?*
2. *Janet and Dave are a married couple with a 6 year old son called Ben. Are they a family?*
3. *Jim and Sue live together with their 6 year old son called Paul. They are not married. Are they a family?*
4. *Sally is divorced with a 10 year old daughter, Karin. Karin lives with Sally. Are these two a family?*
5. *Karin's father, Tom, lives at the other end of the town. Are Karin and Tom a family?*

Children were asked to complete a sheet containing these questions (see Table 2.1) and then they were discussed in groups. Caution needs to be exercised when considering both questionnaire data and the data from group discussions. Firstly, the numbers in the sample are very small. Secondly, when they completed the sheets, there was a good deal of looking over shoulders and whispered discussion. Thirdly, group dynamics worked in different ways, and it only took one confident, strident voice raising points of disagreement to persuade the whole group to change their minds – though, the purpose of the discussions was not to reach consensus. The responses for Village 8–9 year olds were so divergent from Village 10–11 year olds that these have been separated out. Question 2 was the least controversial and all children in the sample counted this nuclear form as 'family'. The following section describes group responses to the other four questions.

On the whole, children's beliefs about what counts as a family appeared to vary according to age and ethnic background. How they varied seemed to centre around whether

Table 2.1   Children's responses to vignette questions, by age and location (percentages for each group)

Response	Village 8–9 year olds (n=28)	Town 8–10 year olds (n=33)	Village 10–11 year olds (n=24)	Village 12–14 year olds (n=43)	Town 12–14 year olds (n=42) (including Pakistani = 11)
Question 1					
Yes	46	49	83	86	38
No	43	48	17	14	60
Don't know	11	3	–	–	2
Question 2					
Yes	100	100	100	100	100
No	–	–	–	–	–
Don't know	–	–	–	–	–
Question 3					
Yes	32	15	92	91	81
No	61	82	8	9	19
Don't know	7	3	–	–	–
Question 4					
Yes	53	18	100	93	55
No	36	79	–	7	43
Don't know	11	3	–	–	2
Question 5					
Yes	54	18	92	88	64
No	39	70	8	9	33
Don't know	7	12	–	3	3

'marriage', 'children' or proximity were the key components of a family. Younger children in particular saw the presence of children and marriage as being necessary to define family, and tended to refer to concrete examples from their own or their kin's situations in discussion. Children of Pakistani origin were particularly likely to describe fathers and other family members as being absent for reasons other than divorce, for example, for work or visits to Pakistan, but these family members still counted as 'family'. In general, older children seemed more likely to generalise beyond their own experiences, without referring to concrete examples. They were also less likely to see 'a family' as depending upon formal contractual relationships, and were more likely to see the nature or quality of the relationships between family members as the defining feature. This was particularly marked in the discussion about absent father and daughter, where the quality of the relationship between father and child, the amount of contact and the precise reason for the absence were emphasised.

Married couple without children

Question 1. John and Susan are a married couple without any children. Are they a family?

Almost exactly half of the younger children, regardless of ethnic background, queried whether a childless married couple counted as a family (see Table 2.1). Roughly half had answered no, and in the discussions, they explained why, 'I said no . . . because they've got no children'. One large group of nine year olds had the following very lively discussion:

> 'NO!' . . . 'they don't have any children' . . . 'not a family without any children' . . . 'No' . . . 'Yes' . . . 'I think maybe' . . . 'I think they're a couple because they're married . . . they're a family . . .'

In this group, the boys were adamant that 'they're not a family because they've got no children . . .'. One girl, Emily, responded: 'If they're married, they're sort of like a family, but because they haven't got any children, they're sort of not like a family, so in some ways they are and in some ways they aren't . . .'.

The youngest children of Pakistani origin were arranged in three groups, two of which broadly agreed with the question,

one group of which had the following discussion: 'No'; 'Yes';
'yes, because they're both married'; 'No'; 'they are only
married, but when they get children, then there's a big
family'. Ten year olds of Pakistani origin seemed more likely
to disagree; because 'children can only make a family';
'because a family needs to have children'. This may reflect
the community from which the children come, in which a
married couple might be likely to be part of an extended
family of parents and other siblings. They would not be
thought of as 'a family' until they themselves had children and
moved out of the family house.

Overall, the importance of self (child) to families is clear in
these younger children's reasons for not counting Question 1
(Q1) as a family.

The Village 10–11 year olds nearly all (83 per cent) saw Q1
as counting as family, as one group commented: 'Yes – 'cos;
like they're close together, they don't have to have children to
have a family, 'cos you've got your mum, relations, your dad,
sisters and brothers'. Similarly, the older Village children
nearly all (86 per cent) agreed with the question. The Town
children were less likely to agree: one girl in one of the groups
said: 'Yeah . . . if they're happy they are'. An argumentative
group of three boys had the following discussion:

> Tim: No, no they're not, 'cos they ain't got no children, how
> can they be a family? (crossly)
> John: But they don't need children to be a family.
> Mark: They do!
> Tim: They're just a couple though, ain't they, there's only
> two of them.

In a group of five boys of Pakistani origin, one boy said 'No,
they're not a family, because they've got no children'; another
hesitated, and said [yes], ''cos they're married'. In one group
of girls, Vicky said, 'Yeah, I think they are'; another girl in the
same group said 'they're more of a couple really, they are. A
family depends on kids and kids depend on them'. In other
groups all agreed that they were a family. It is difficult to
explain why the Town sample were less likely to see this
configuration as a family. There may be a number of reasons
for this: their responses may reflect situations where couples
marry because of children, again reflecting the centrality of
children to families; or they may have been reflecting on their
own situations and experiences.

In summary, for about half the younger children, and more than half of the older Town children, the presence of children was important to their constructions of what counts as a family. This was much less likely to be the case for the older Village children. There were no marked differences according to ethnic background and gender.

Cohabiting couple with a child

Question 3. Jim and Sue live together with their 6 year old son called Paul. They are not married. Are they a family?

This question, relating to non-marital childrearing and cohabitation, tended not to count as family for the youngest children (regardless of ethnic background), but it did for most of the older children (see Table 2.1). Many children said they were 'sort of' a family. One large group of nine-year-old children had the following discussion. Many of the children said 'no', but some said 'yes'. One girl said 'They're sort of like a family'. Another said 'No, they're just boyfriend and girlfriend'. A boy responded by saying, 'But if they have children, then they're a family, aren't they'. Georgina said: 'They aren't married, so it in't a family, in't a family'. The discussion then went as follows:

> Emily: You don't have to be married to be like a family, like, you know, I mean, they might not have enough money to get married, or they can't be bothered to organise anything, in case they might want to get divorced and that costs a lot of money and then it would be a waste of money and a waste of time.
>
> Betty: My auntie isn't married, and she's got some children . . .
>
> Emma: My auntie, well she went off with loads of boys, one of them she had a baby with, and they didn't get married, because Auntie [name], she knew that she wouldn't be able to stay with [baby]'s (my cousin's) dad, he sees her like at the weekend, and like I said to my auntie 'are you a family?', she goes 'we're sort of a family'.
>
> Another girl: 'My auntie well she's got my cousin [name] and she weren't married until she got a man'.
>
> Emily: 'Babies change lots of things, don't they?'

One boy said 'they might get married, [and then] they will be a family. But they're not a family yet'. Marriage appears to be an important element in these younger children's definitions of family.

Village 10–11 year olds mostly said yes, some qualified their answers by saying things like 'yes, yeah, in a way, well, they are really, 'cos they've got a child'. One girl, Jade, whose parents had divorced, said of her mother's new partner, 'even though . . . he lives with my mum, we're like a family'. In one of the groups there was the following discussion between two boys: Barney: 'I don't think so, because they're not married'. Richard: 'They live together, and they love each other, doesn't mean they have to be married, they might not have enough money to get married'.

The 10 year olds of Pakistani origin put far more emphasis on marriage and mostly (82 per cent) did not count a cohabiting couple with a child as a family, saying, for example, 'They have to be married', 'No, they are not a family because they are not married – they have got a family but not close family, but cut in the middle, then you fix the part together and you make a whole part'. As noted above, such a relationship would be against cultural norms in their community of origin, and this is reflected in their responses.

Among some groups of older Village children, there was very little discussion. With the Town 14 year olds there was a range of responses: 'Yeah . . . [it] doesn't matter if you're married, it doesn't mean that you're not a family' (girl). In one group of boys there was the following interchange:

> Tim: No, 'cos they're not married, are they?
> John: You don't have to be married.
> Tim: You do!
> John: You don't!
> Tim: It would be weird, wouldn't it, if you weren't married?

Other comments were: 'No, well, they are kind of, because if they've had a child' and 'actually, you get married to have a family'. A group of 13-year-old boys of Pakistani origin had some discussion: Waqas: 'they're still a family'; Others: 'No, they're not'; Wyed: 'because they've got children as well'.

In summary, the younger children were more likely to see marriage as necessary to define a family regardless of ethnic background. The older children seemed to have more flexible rules than the younger children in this respect.

Lone mother and daughter

Question 4. Sally is divorced with a 10 year old daughter, Karin. Karin lives with Sally. Are these two a family?

This question, related to lone motherhood, and Table 2.1 shows that youngest Village children were slightly more likely (53 per cent) to consider this configuration as family, while the children of Pakistani origin were not (79 per cent). In the older groups, there were again differences between Town and Village children in their responses to this question. One nine-year-old boy asked for the meaning of the word 'divorce'; another girl in the group explained 'it's when you split up'. (In other groups, children appeared to be familiar with the term, and the bilingual children did not hesitate to ask the meaning of a word if they weren't sure.) For these younger children the quality of the relationship was important, as this extract shows:

> Charlotte: If they get on, and the parents still get on, and they can still be friends, then yes, they could be a family, but if they don't get on, and they can't bear to see the sight of each other, then, no, but with a child that is a family . . . maybe.

> Emily: Well, they're sort of like a family, because mother and child live together, but they're sort of not like a family because the dad doesn't live with them . . .

> Sam: Yes, if you're divorced, you're still a family . . .

In a group of four ten year old boys of Pakistani origin, one boy said 'they are a family because they both were married and had a child, but then they had a divorce, so they've just "played up" but they are still a family . . . miss, the one's with the child is a family . . .'.

In the older groups, there were again differences between Town and Village children in their responses to this question. In the groups of older Village children, there was virtually no discussion and nearly all (93 per cent) counted this as family. In one group, however, Danielle said: 'I don't think they're a family because the dad's missing'. Robert responded: 'it doesn't make any difference . . .' and Danielle replied: 'it doesn't make it a whole family, it makes it part of a family'. Just over half the older Town children counted it as a family. In two different groups of 13 year old girls, two girls expressed quite a 'traditional' view: 'no . . . the husband's gone, and you need a husband and wife to bring up a child'. In response to another girl saying 'but there's a kid and a mum, it's still a family', one girl said: 'yeah, it usually takes three to be a family'.

In summary, younger children were less likely to perceive a single mother and a child as a family, and this was particularly marked among the children of Pakistani origin, and reflects the unlikelihood of this type of relationship existing in their community. However, the older Town children were also quite likely not to see this configuration as counting as family.

Separated father and daughter

Question 5. Karin's father, Tom, lives at the other end of the town. Are Karin and Tom a family?

The final question intended to explore whether or not an absent father counts as 'family', and led to a range of responses across the ages of the children concerned. In their questionnaire answers, the same proportion of the youngest children counted this configuration as family as counted Q4 as family. In the older Town sample, more children saw this as family than saw divorced mum and daughter as family (see Table 2.1).

In the youngest age group of Village children, there was the following discussion: Girl: 'I'm a family and I don't live with my dad . . .' Boy: 'I don't agree . . . because they're divorced'. In another group one girl disagreed, saying 'No, because they don't live together, they live in different directions'. The large group of nine year olds had the following discussion:

No! Yes! Maybe! Shouts: They're not!

Keri: I think they are, because if they still see each other, at the weekends or in the school holidays, then yes, but if they don't then they might be, but not as much as they used to be, because they were family at one point, and they can still carry on being a family, even if they are divorced . . .

Sam: Well, no, because this family won't be living together.

Kevin: But if you're family, 'cos you've got aunts and uncles and you don't live together, you don't live in the same house as them . . .

Betty: I think they are a family because even if the mum and dad don't love each other, the dad and the child, or the mum and the child, love each other. If the child thinks it's a family, it's gonna make them happier.

Emma: I said yes, because if they still see each other, they're still part of a family . . . it depends on whether the person likes you or not . . . you could like the person, not love the person . . .

Emily: Well, I think they're sort of like a family, because if Karin goes to see her dad, then they are still a family, they're sort of like a family in one way, and sort of not like a family because they don't live with each other.

These girls are highlighting the nature of the relationship between father and daughter as defining whether or not they are 'a family'; in other words, it depends on how they feel about each other.

For the youngest children of Pakistani origin, there was a mix of yes/no responses and not much discussion. One boy said, 'no, because they are divorced . . .'; in another group, a child said 'yes, yes they are, but they live in different houses. Miss, some people don't want to live with their family'. When this question was discussed with ten year olds of Pakistani origin, some children interpreted it as being quite separate from the question about the lone mother, and saw whether or not this counted as family as depending on the reason why the father was absent. One girl mentioned that 'some of your family can be in Pakistan but they are still your family', and this came up in other groups too, for example, a group of four boys said the following: 'Yeah, yes, maybe . . . it doesn't matter, he's always [her] father, no matter where they were'; 'you're still a family, like my dad goes somewhere else, we're still a family though . . .'. In another group of boys, one asked 'are they separated?' Another boy answered: 'No, they only live apart'. Another boy said: 'he might be going for a job somewhere, Miss, if he is gone for a job then that is family, but if he's slipped up with his wife, then that isn't a family . . . If they both love each other then it's still a family. If they're somewhere else and you're somewhere else, you're still a family'.

For the 10–11 year old Village children, there was very little discussion about this question and most responded 'yes'. For example, one girl said 'Yes, to be a family you don't have to live together, he's still her dad', and Jade said, 'cos we don't live with my Nana but we're still a family'. In another group one boy said: 'yes, because that's her dad', but there was some disagreement:

Richard: I don't know, I think it's quite a difficult one.

Louisa: Well, they're about the same because one's the father and one's the mother, so they're both a family, whatever one they're with.

Richard: They're still family aren't they? I wonder what Dannie would think.

Here Richard is referring to one of his classmates who he knows is in a single-parent family, who had written about how she hardly sees her father. In the group discussion, she did not see this configuration as a family: she said 'no, . . . because Karin and Tom don't really see each other that often, they don't live with them . . . 'cos there's me, my mum, and my brother, and my dad lives at the other end of [large city 60-odd miles away] so I wouldn't really class it as a family if he doesn't live with us'. Kathie qualified this, saying 'but Tom lives at the other end of town, so he's not that far away'; in doing so she seems to be linking physical proximity with emotional contact.

With the older Village children, they nearly all agreed that absent father did count as family and there was virtually no discussion. The one exception was Danielle, who said 'they could claim they're a family, but they're not a close family', and Simon added: 'if they love each other, then they're a family, doesn't make any difference'.

Older Village children tended to see Q5 as following on from Q4, but the Town children did not, and this may partly explain their contradictory responses to Q4 and Q5. As noted above, Q4 had the word 'divorce' as the reason for the separation, while Q5 did not, and the word 'divorce' may have negative connotations. In the Town groups there were several examples of the children querying why the father lived separately from the daughter, and the children did not automatically assume that the parents were divorced: for example, in a group of 13 year olds, one girl asked 'are they together, are they? or do they live apart?'; another girl replied: 'No, because they don't live together, even though she's his daughter'. A third said 'but she could go and see him?'. In a group of five boys of Pakistani origin, one boy said 'they are a family'. Another boy said: 'I don't think they are a family'. A third boy said: 'they are! they're married, he might have gone to work'; 'it's whether they're divorced'; another said 'all our uncles and that live away, but they're still a family'. These responses highlight how the notion of 'fatherlessness' as relating to divorce is essentially a white, European construct. In minority ethnic communities significant male figures (fathers or uncles) are often absent because of work reasons (or because of immigration controls) and the children's responses reflect this.

In another group of older children, one girl said 'even though they don't live together, they're still a family'. A mixed group gave the following responses: 'yeah', 'no, 'cos they don't live together'; 'they're all split up'; 'there's not much of a connection'; 'I think families are together', 'dad could go on a business trip'. One girl said 'it depends on the circumstances, if they live 50/50 then they are a family, but if she only goes at weekends, they aren't a family'. The amount of contact was what defined family for her.

In summary, younger children were less likely to see this configuration as a family, and this was particularly the case for children of Pakistani origin, though in discussion the fact that fathers are often absent because they work away from home emerged repeatedly. Older children were more likely to count lone father and daughter as family. Overall, in discussions, the importance of the quality of the relationship between father and child, the amount of contact, and the reason for the absence were emphasised.

Summary

In conclusion, even though many of the children saw marriage, children, and co-residence as necessary components of a 'family', there were several young children who did not. Thus, although the nuclear norm is expressed, even younger children can consider alternative family forms as 'family'. This came through quite clearly in the group discussions where children were able to reflect upon, and discuss these ideas, rather than answer a simple closed question. When data from group discussions are considered in conjunction with their responses to the open-ended questions a more complex picture emerges, in that it is not merely the structure or the nature of the contract (that is, children or marriage) that makes a family, but the roles and relationships involved in family life, and the provision of emotional and material security. This is explored in the following section.

3. Definitions of family: parents

This section explores children's responses to the questions 'what is a family?' and 'what are families for?'. Many of the children's definitions reflected their accounts of who is important to them personally. They tended to define 'family' in broadly similar ways to how they described what their families' members, but especially their parents, do for them. 'Mum and dad', or 'parents' or 'my family' were mentioned by nearly all children in the sample (only six children did not). In terms of **who** the children drew, wrote about or mapped as important, children of all ages described a wide range of people – mostly parents and siblings, but also grandparents, great grandparents, aunts, uncles, cousins, stepparents, step-siblings. The focus is on the meaning of the abstract concept of 'family', as expressed by children, and children's (concrete) descriptions of who is important to them. In other words, it contrasts expressed beliefs with the realities of relationships in practice (see Finch and Mason, 1993).

The emphasis in the accounts from younger children was on being provided for and cared for by parents, and this seems to be the case across gender and ethnic background. Gender roles within the household were clearly differentiated, particularly by the children of Pakistani origin. Older children's accounts were longer and included more variation, but the quality of the relationships remained central: love, care and mutual support are the key constituents of families. While some children used the term 'related' and notions of relatedness to describe families, they were not necessarily taking related to mean 'biological connectedness' and some were clear that people are linked to each other in different ways, through marriage as well as blood ties. Rather, caring and love, and the quality of the relationships involved, and fulfilling roles, defined family, and this was clear across age, gender and ethnicity.

Three themes were clear in the children's definitions: the roles (or functions) of family members (in other words, care, provision and nurturing); relationships (love and affection), and household structure ('mum and dad and children', or more commonly, 'a group of people who are related' or 'who live together'). All children, regardless of age, gender or ethnic origin, mentioned one, both, or all three of these features in various combinations in their definitions of family. Figures 3.1 and 3.2 show the distribution of children's responses according to gender, age, and ethnicity. The following sections discuss examples of each of these combinations of themes.

Structure

Very few children (n=5) defined families only by structure, and they were very unlikely to define a family in terms of the stereotypical image of two parents and children, for example:

> A family is something with a group of 4, 5, 6, 7, 8, 9, 10 people. [*What are families for?*] Families are to have children. (Laura, 8)

> A family is related to each other. They could be a mom, dad, brother(s) or sister(s). People also that are related to you like grandad/mother, uncles, aunts or cousins could be a family. (Malik, 14)

Roles

Younger children were more likely than older children to write about how they themselves were materially and physically provided for by parents, and the roles parents played in looking after them. For example:

> A family is people who care for you. Families are for looking after you. (Kyle, 8)

The roles that family members play in providing for children were reflected in written accounts of who is important to them:

> My mum and dad and sister are important, because they do things for me, like buy me sweets and fizzy drinks and biscuits. (Susie, 8)

> My mum and dad are important to me. Because they care for us and mums make food for us and dads bring food for us, and

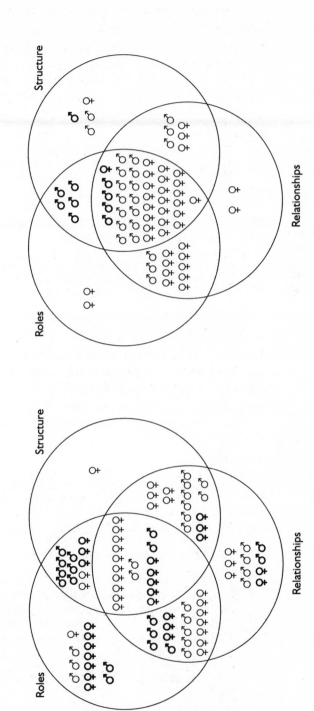

Figure 3.1   Children's responses to 'what is a family?' and 'what are families for?' coded by theme, 8–11 year olds, children of Pakistani origin in bold, ♂ – male, ♀ – female

Figure 3.2   Children's responses to 'what is a family?' and 'what are families for?' coded by theme, 12–14 year olds, children of Pakistani origin in bold, ♂ – male, ♀ – female

when we get hurt and cut our knees and when we cry they make us cheer up. (Shamila, 8)

My mum is important to me because she looks after me and does the housework and helps me to find things when I have lost them. My dad is important to me because he looks after me and brings me things to play with and to eat. My dad gives me presents and things to play with on my birthday and on Eid. (Kussum, 10)

When you go home from school, they give you things, they let you go to play cricket, give me money to go shops, buy some things, to buy lots of things. (Mohbeen, 9)

For some of the youngest children of Pakistani origin, members of the extended family were there to look after them when their parents were away:

families are for you, so if your mum and dad go to Pakistan or another country, the other half or the other quarter or something can like, look after you. (Tahir, 8)

On the whole, children of all ages and regardless of ethnic background described who does what in the household in terms of the gendered division of labour, and this extended to the provision of emotional support in families. Mothers are clearly important to children, especially girls, for 'listening' to their problems and several girls described how they could talk to their mothers 'about anything' (see also Duncombe and Marsden, 1993; O'Brien and Jones, 1996; Ribbens, 1994). For example:

My mum is important to me because I can always tell her all my secrets and she will always stick by me. (Lisa, 13)

My mum is very important to me because we care for each other, she helps me get through bad patches. Me and my mum respect each other. (Janine, 13)

The most important person to me is my step-mum because I can tell her more things than I can with my real mum. The reason I can tell my step-mum more is because I don't see my real mum very often because my mum and dad are split up. But I still love my mum and dad just as much as I do my step-mum. (Caroline, 12)

Boys, on the other hand, tended to describe 'doing things' with fathers:

My mum and dad are important to me because they are my parents. My mum is important because she cooks me food and [does the] washing. My dad is important to me because he takes me to work with him so I get to go on roofs at people's houses. (Mark, 13)

A further theme in the accounts from the older children was that of mutual support. In their definitions of what families are for, nearly a half of the older children used terms like 'families are for caring for each other', 'sharing', and 'looking after each other'. Several mentioned how they do things for other members of their families, and there were two instances of 14 year olds, one girl and one boy, describing how they were helping their mothers who both had knee injuries. Another boy mentioned how the most important person to him is his dad, a lone parent:

because he is the only parent I have got left and he struggles to look after me so I help as well. He is very caring. (Jack, 14)

Relationships

Some (11 of the younger, 2 of the older, see Figures 3.1 and 3.2) children defined family only in terms of the quality of relationships, and the love and affection that family members provide to each other, for example:

A family is loving people. Families are for telling people secrets and they care about you. (Georgina, 9)

Families are for helping each other and loving each other. (Inzaman, 10)

A family is people you love. Families are for love and looking after each other. (Max, 11)

A family is people who love each other. People can do things together and tell secrets to each other. People who care for each other. Families are for loving each other. (Cher, 13)

Structure and roles

In practice, these themes merged in most children's accounts in various ways, for example:

A family is made up of people who support you. Everybody is born with a family. Families are for helping you out. (Zoe, 12)

The small number of older children of Pakistani origin who defined family held very similar views, and their definitions centred around family structure and roles:

> A family is a group of people living together, parents and children. Families are for helping you out and you are not alone, grow you up. (Saeed, 12)

> A family is who cares about each other, and people who are related to you. (Imran, 14)

Roles and relationships

Notions of provision, help, care and support (that is, roles and relationships) were central in the definitions from the younger children of Pakistani origin: 'Families are for making people feel unlonely. They feed, help you' (Shazia). One boy expanded his definitions of what families are for to include 'who expect you to get a good education and look after them when they are older' (Ali, 11), reflecting a strong sense of family obligations. Another boy, Imran, defined family as 'A family is being together, helping each other, sticking up for each other, and telling what's right or wrong'. The notion of love and support also appears in accounts of who is important to them:

> My mum is important to me because she feeds me and clothes me and loves me very much. My dad is important to me because he pays for the food I eat and the clothes I wear. He cares for me and loves me very much. (Nadia, 9)

> My dad is the best thing in the whole of my life because [he is] kind and he cares about me and he loves me. Same with the rest of my family. (Jabraan, 10)

The children of Pakistani origin wrote in terms of a clear division of labour within the household along the lines of gender, in that mothers cared for children and provided them with food, while fathers go out to work to get 'money so we can buy food'.

Some of the older children (regardless of ethnic background) also defined family in terms of roles and relationships:

> Families are for help, mental and physical stability, love, support. (Alvin, 14)

> A family is someone who is always there for you, a family you can trust, love, comfort and talk to. A family is always there to love, and to do things together. (Eve, 14)

> A family is somewhere you are loved, wanted and spend time with, care for you and brought you into the world, important. Families are for love, homes, helping you, understanding problems. (Danielle, 13)

and this was reflected in some accounts of who is important:

> My mum because she takes care of me and I love her very much. She is the most important person in my life at the moment. My mum's boyfriend is important to me because he helps my mum and me and my brother a lot. (Charlotte, 13)

Relationships and structure

For some children, family or household structure combined with the quality of the relationships were the defining characteristics of family. For example:

> A family is someone who cares about you and lives with you. Families are for helping and caring, loving too. (Nadiya, 10)

> It's normally a group of three or more people with a mum and a dad and some children, and who love and care for one another . . . usually. Most of the time you live with a family. (Betty, 9)

> A family is a group of people who love you. Families are for loving you and for being kind to you. (James, 10)

The youngest children of Pakistani origin defined families in very similar ways to the Village children, though there were differences in vocabulary. They tended not to use the word 'love', for example:

> A family is someone who you live with, and who you really like, you do everything with, you live round their house and everything like that. (Shareen, 8)

Later in the discussion, she expanded this and said: 'not who you only like, who you *really, really* like'. These children used words like respect and trust as well as care, for example: 'your family cares about you'.

Structure, roles, and relationships

On the whole, older children were more likely to give more detail and more complicated definitions, and as Figure 3.2 shows, nearly half of them (n=42) included all three themes (roles, responsibilities and structure) in their definitions.

There were no clear differences according to gender. Some of the older children mentioned 'related', but in the context of love and care:

> A family is a group of people who are related and love each other. Families are for caring for each other. (Mulder, 12)

> A family is a mum a dad and children or boyfriend girlfriend and child and they look after you well, and a good relationship. Families are for to bring people together and have to give love to something you brought into the world like a child. Something you and your partner has made and have a family. (Geri, 13)

> A family is a group of people who are related who respect, love and value one another. Families are for helping you through bad times, cheering you up when you feel down. Caring for one another! (Nisa, 13)

On the other hand, some specified that a family did not necessarily have to be related by birth:

> A family is related to me in some way. Mum, dad, grandparents, brothers, sisters, aunts, uncles, cousins, half-brothers/sisters, stepsisters/brothers are all family. Families are for giving me stuff; food, clothes, presents. Loving, caring for me and for giving things back to. And for people to talk to. (Bob, 14)

About a quarter (n=19) of the younger children included all three themes as defining family, as Figure 3.1 shows, for example:

> I think a family is something of a group of people, it can be three, or more, or less, it doesn't matter how many amount of people you have, but a family is some people who love and care about you and they'll always love and care about you, it doesn't matter what happens, they'll always care about you. (Keri, 9)

> A family is someone or a group of people who love and care for you and look after you. Families are for helping us when we grow up. (Louisa, 11)

> I think a family is something that is a group of people who love and care for each other, and help when their life hurts. (Emma, 9)

Happy families?

One dominant notion about families is that, like childhood, they are supposed to be happy (Holland, 1992; Ennew and

Milne, 1989). Most of the definitions of family and accounts of who is important from the younger children were very positive. A small number of older children did reflect this notion of happy families and the nuclear form:

> A family is a mum and dad with children who are happy together and whose parents are not split up. (Dougie, 12)

One 13 year old girl who described living with her mum wrote: 'I'm glad my dad doesn't live with us because we wouldn't be happy. My view of a family is where everyone's happy'. Other older children clearly expressed a different and perhaps more realistic view that families can still be families even if they don't always get on together:

> A family is a group of people which all care about each other. They can all cry together, laugh together, argue together and go through all the emotions together. Some live together as well. Families are for helping each other through life. (Tara, 13)

> A family is a small community living together not always getting on. Families are for talking to, making dinner, looking after you. (Ross, 13)

> I can't describe what a family is. Everybody has one, you're just born into it. You argue sometimes, have fun, go on holiday, but I don't know what it is. I know you usually have mum, dad, brother, sister, gran, grandad, aunts, uncles, cousins. Families are so you're not lonely, they are also there to bring you to life. (Rosie, 13)

> A family is 2 parents, some kids, that can work together to live a happy life. (Anita, 14)

This example shows that for Anita, the notion that families are happy is not a 'given', it is something that has to be thought about and worked upon. Some of the older children did express some ambivalence towards their parents:

> My mum and dad are very important to me as they help me if I have a problem, and they look after me. Sometimes I don't like them because they tell me off even though I have not done anything wrong. (Stephanie, 13)

> I can't stand being grounded because if I don't go out then I get quite unpleasant! So therefore I'm always good. Well, that's what my mum thinks. If she knew some of the things I get up to she'd have a fit! Everything I do is legal! (Louise, 13)

> My dad . . . because I don't get along with him at all, so I want to be able to get along with him. My mum because she is always there for me when I need her most (my dad is also there for me, but we have a tendency to argue a lot at home). (Callum, 12)

> My whole family are important. I sometimes don't like my mum and dad but I always love them. (Theodore, 13)

One girl (Melanie, 13) wrote: 'families are for caring and being happy with each other', and in her description of who is important, had commented: 'I can get on with my family, i.e. Mum, dad and 2 sisters better because my parents are not divorced. I think it would be harder if they were split up', showing that some children see divorce as problematic.

Summary

The focus, then, in most of the younger children's accounts was on what families do for children in terms of provision of material and emotional support. Older children were likely to define families as doing things for each other and providing mutual support. Generally, children's definitions of family reflected their descriptions of who is important to them, and there was very little discrepancy between how they described their own families and how they defined families in general. When they said what they thought a family is and what families are for, it was clear that love, care and mutual respect and support were the key characteristics for them of 'family', and this was the case regardless of gender, ethnic background and location. Overall, children's definitions did not centre around the 'nuclear norm'. For many children, 'family' consists of a wide range of people, and it is the roles that these people perform, and the quality of the relationships, that define them as 'family'.

4. Who is important to me?: siblings, kin, friends and others

This section discusses children's accounts of a range of significant others: brothers and sisters, kin relations, friends, pets and religious figures, and gives an indication of the wider context of the children's lives. As we have seen, the presence of children and wider kin is a characteristic of families for many children (many wrote that a family is a 'group of people who are related'). Alongside their descriptions of family members, their accounts of who is important to them also highlighted how central a range of significant others are to them as providers of companionship and emotional support. Friendships were more important for older children, both boys and girls. For Muslim children, religion and religious figures are central. For other children, their pets are important as a source of companionship and are seen as part of their families.

Siblings

The presence of children is a characteristic of families for some children, as we saw in Chapter 2. Twenty-three per cent (n=43) specifically mentioned children in their definitions. Many children also drew their brothers and/or sisters and mentioned them in descriptions of who is important. Sibling relationships are clearly important to children and this may be masked by a tendency in psychological research to focus on parent/mother-child dyads when there may in fact be important triadic (or more) relationships within families, but it is important to see children's relationships in the wider context of their links with a range of family members (Dunn 1993).

Some children only provided drawings, and did not give written accounts, and there are more data from the children of Pakistani origin than the Village children, and more from girls than boys. With one exception (Zafran, below), the comments by children of Pakistani origin about their siblings were positive:

> My big sister is important to me because she helps me to do the housework and takes me to the library and takes me to [place name]. My other sisters are important to me because they help me with my work and take me to places and are helpful to me. My brother is important to me because he goes out and earns money. (Kusum, 10)

> My big sister is important to me because she helps me on my home work and sometimes on my reading books. (Wassim, 10)

> I always be sad because my brothers hit me . . . One day when I went to seaside my brothers buried me in the sand. (Zafran, 10)

Two differences are noticeable between the accounts of children of Pakistani origin and other children's accounts. Firstly, some of the children of Pakistani origin described large families, almost hierarchically arranged in age order, for example:

> My brother (big) is important to me because without him I would not be able to do my work. My sister (big) is important to me because without her I could not do the housework . . . My little sister is important to me because without her I would have nothing to do. My little brother is important to me because without him I would have no-one to play with. My littlest sister is important to me because she always makes something for me to do. (Shazia, 10)

Secondly, Shazia's description (above) may also illustrate a preference for (or practice of) playing with siblings among families of Pakistani origin. The obligations of family members may emphasise the rights and responsibilities of older children to care for younger siblings. This is reflected in other accounts, for example:

> My baby sister is important to me because she is smaller than me and I got every right to look after her . . . My brothers are important to me because I will not have anyone to play with. (Nakila, 11)

> My sister is important to me because without her it would be boring. (Ali, 11)

It is possible that family members provide the most likely source of companionship for children of Pakistani origin, and this is confirmed in research with adults. Saifullah Khan (1979) notes that 'the closest bonds of friendship and emotional attachment are within the family and close kin' (p. 44).

Mostly the older children wrote very positively about their siblings, and some described how they provide support to each other:

> My sister helps me with what I look like when I go to parties. She's pregnant at the moment so her baby is very important to me. If my sister goes through any distress I cheer her up. (Tara, 13)

> My sister is my twin and we take care of [each other]. (Geri, 13)

> My brother and sister [are important] as we do things for each other and do things together. (Fred, 14)

Step-siblings were included here by some children, for example:

> My sister is important too and my stepbrother and sister are too. (Sophie, 13)

> My step-brother is very important to me as when I have problems he really does care and stick up for me. When we were younger we used to fight but now we're more grown up we can be really close. (Danielle, 13)

At the same time there were some examples of more conflictual relationships with siblings, but these were usually qualified by an indication that the children 'love them really'. For example:

> My brother is [important] too, although I don't say it because we're always fighting, but I don't think I could live without him. (Charlotte, 13)

> My little sister is important to me because I can sometimes trust her. She does get very annoying, though. (Callum, 12)

In summary, the relationship between siblings frequently involves rivalry and fighting, but is also underpinned by a good deal of mutual affection, and in some cases siblings clearly provide an important source of support to each other. These accounts also suggest that there may be different cultural expectations about sibling relationships.

Other kin

The assumption is often made that western families have become increasingly isolated and dispersed because of migration patterns, with the consequence that kin ties are no longer as significant as they used to be (see for example Skolnick, 1991 for USA; Morgan, 1996). However, research based on adults' accounts of family relationships is challenging this (see Finch and Mason, 1993; McGlone, Park and Roberts, 1996/7; Scott, 1997). Children's perspectives on family life also suggest that these assumptions need to be questioned. As the previous section showed, children often defined families as including a range of kin. They also described kin in their accounts of who is important to them. Some children mentioned specific members of their extended family in more detail, and this was the case not only for the children of Pakistani origin (as one might have assumed), but also for the other children. Younger children of Pakistani origin did not tend to describe wider kin (only two ten-year-olds mentioned grandparents, for example). On the other hand, aunts and uncles and especially 'Aunties' were markedly important in the lives of some of these children, and this may reflect migration patterns in which members of parents' generation migrated together, while grandparents remain in Pakistan. It may also reflect mutual obligations of family members to care for each other:

> My auntie is important because I sleep with her, I stay with her, I go to town with her. Wherever she go I go with her. When she went to Pakistan I could not go with her because it was my hospital [appointment]. (Fatemah, 8)

> My auntie is important to me because she takes me to the shop. My uncle is important to me because he takes me to the park. (Erin, 10)

Several younger Village children mentioned specific kin, for example, 'Auntie [name] is also important to me because she is nice to me' (Laura, 8); and nearly all the children included kin in their drawings and lists of who was important. Some of the Junior school children included kin in their written accounts:

> I have a nanna and grandad which are really nice, and I have another nanna and grandad, they are also nice. I have two aunties from different sides of the family and one uncle from my mum's side of the family. (Jade, 11)

> My mum, dad, sister, brother-in-law, and nephews are always
> important to me because no matter what they're always there
> for me. (Louisa, 11)

Some older children (about a third of the girls, and a fifth of
the boys) specifically mentioned a range of kin, uncles, aunts,
cousins, nieces, nephews, great grandparents, even god-
parents, for example:

> Uncle [is important to me] because he is funny and kind to me.
> (Frank, 12)

> My grandma and grandad are important to me because they
> are very good at listening, which I like. (Dougie, 12)

> All my cousins (girl aged 18, boy aged 5, girl aged 4, and girl)
> are special to me but my two youngest cousins (boy aged 5 and
> girl aged 4) are really special because I go around their house,
> everyday after school I see them, so I have seen them grow up.
> (Shannon, 13)

> My nan is very important as all my other grandparents have
> died. My godparents are important too as they are the ones
> who have to take responsibility for me if my parents die . . . My
> nephew is very important to me as well as now I am an auntie
> and I now help to look after him. (Sophie, 13)

> My grandad, he is my favourite relative other than my parents
> I am his only granddaughter so he spoils me a bit. My gran, I
> stop at her house everyday after school to see her and as above
> she spoils me a bit. My grandad, he only has me and my
> brother to spoil and I see him every week. (Christina, 13)

These examples of children mentioning kin show that some
children have regular contact with extended family members,
regardless of ethnic background. However, the research
methods were ethnocentric, and using different tools might
have led Pakistani children to describe the biraderi system
described in Section 1. As we have seen, there were many
similarities, as well as differences, in the white children's
definitions of family and in those of the children of Pakistani
origin. This may reflect changing patterns of kinship among
British Asians. Both Dosanjh and Ghuman (1996) in their
study of childrearing practices among Punjabis, and Modood,
Beishon and Virdee (1994) drawing on 1991 Census data, note
the movement away from extended family systems among
South Asian families in the UK:

For Asians the two-adults-plus-children household has become the most common way of living, being more than twice as common among Asians as the national average . . . it also marks something of an irony than Asians now exhibit most clearly a form of family . . . that is or used to be regarded as quintessentially western. (Modood, Beishon and Virdee, 1994, p. 33)

However, this does not mean that roles and responsibilities in Pakistani families are similar to those within white European nuclear families, because traditional notions of interdependence and the importance of the family unit are still likely to take priority over individualism, and notions of family obligations and reciprocities are likely to be very strong (see Ahmad, 1996; Dosanjh and Ghuman, 1996). Further, as Ahmad notes, 'there is diversity of experiences and expectations within the Asian communities, as well as similarities between the Asian and other communities' (Ahmad, 1996, pp. 71–2).

Children's friendships: 'friend', 'best friend', 'very best friend'

There is a large amount of research on children's friendships, mainly from the perspective of developmental psychology (for example Rubin, 1981; Berndt and Ladd, 1989) which tends to emphasise the importance of friendship for individual development and how this relates to adult sociability. Previous research has emphasised how older children often spend more time with their friends than they do with their families, and this tendency increases with age (O'Brien and Jones, 1997; Griffiths, 1995; Hey, 1997; James, 1996). The fact that friendships clearly become increasingly central to children's social lives was reflected in some of the children's accounts, for example:

> Well, my family I suppose are important to me. Although on an average day I spend more time with my friends . . . My friends of which there are ten all aged between 12 and 20. They are all important to me, very important to me, I spend more time with them than anyone else, as soon as I get home from school it's homework, dinner then out with them till 9 p.m., then some more time to stay out if I'm lucky. (Louise, 13)

On the whole, in the younger Village sample about half the girls and a quarter of the boys mentioned their friends. This is in contrast with the subsample of children of Pakistani origin, in which only three boys mentioned friends, though this may also reflect the way the children interpreted the question 'who is important to me?', but may also relate to cultural specificity of the notion 'friendship'. The question was deliberately open, but it is striking that so many children did mention their friends, given that the project was about 'family'. Geographical location may also be a factor here, in that rural children may have a more limited pool of friends to draw upon, and this may well increase the importance of their pets to them.

Particularly in the older age group, friends were important in both Village and Town samples. Just under half (20/44) of the boys and nearly two-thirds of the girls (25/42) in this older age group mentioned friends. There were differences in the way girls and boys described their friendships: girls tended to describe close friends or 'best friends', rather than groups of friends, and were particularly expansive about their friendships, for example:

> [friends] because they have always been there for me and I love them, just know that they are there to help cheer up, comfort when going through a bad time. (Louisa, 11)

> My best friend [name] from where I used to live is very important to me because when I am feeling down she is on the phone cheering me up. (Biz, 11; she had described how her father was dead.)

> My friends are very important to me and they help me with problems and they help me with homework. I have got lots of best friends [list of eight girls' names]. So I really am lucky to be part of such a big group. I need friends around because they support me and never criticise me and I then have people to hang around with and do things with. (Shannon, 13)

This theme of uncritical support, trust, and 'being there' for you is one that emerged repeatedly in the girls' accounts. The girls nearly always describe same-sex friendships, often using kin terms to describe the closeness of the relationship:

> My best friend [girl] is important to me as she understands me for who I am and no matter what I go through she always sticks by me. She is very caring and loving to me and through being the only child I always feel that I have *an older sister* because that is what she's like. (Danielle, 13, emphasis added)

Two girls described close relationships, comparable to family relationships, with older female friends:

> My next door neighbour is important to me because if I can't tell my mum something I can always tell her. She is like *my second mum*. Also my next door neighbour has twins, they're very special to me because *they are like my brother and sister* I will never have. (Janine, 13, emphasis added)

> My friend . . . is the second most [important] because *she is like a mum to me* and I see her a lot. She is nice to me and she is very friendly. I like her a lot and I can tell her everything I want, she is 30. My mum is the 1st important she takes care of me and I love her. (Geri, 13, emphasis added)

The assumption is often made that boys' friendships fulfil a different function to those of girls, that of active contributions, like sticking up for each other, and doing things together (like fathers and sons), and there were examples of this:

> My friends like me because when we have fights we jump in for each other. (Wassim, 10)

> My best friend [boy] in [nearby large town] is important to me because I can always have a laugh with him and play football and basketball. (Dougie, 12)

However, some of the boys also described how their friends are important for them because they listened, were loyal and could be trusted:

> All the people who are in my form are important but especially [2 boys, 1 girl], [boy] is special to me because if I tell him a secret he keeps it, [girl] is very important because she helps me with my problems and cares for people. (Christian, 12)

> My friends are very important to me but one friend in particular. He always listens to me and I can trust him not to tell anyone. He is always [underlined 3 times] there for me. He is a very dear friend. (Callum, 12)

> My friends are also very important to me because they are there when I need them they cheer me up they help me when I get stuck. They understand and try and help me if I have something wrong. They don't moan at me if I don't get something right. (Paul, 13)

> My friends are important to me . . . My friends always listen to me and help me. [boy] is my best buddy because he listens to me on and off for ten years. I stick up for him and buy him biscuits because he is always skint. (Alvin, 14)

To some extent, boys are using a different language – of sticking up for each other, having fun together, but they also use the notion of uncritical support, in a similar way to girls.

In summary, friendship becomes increasingly important as children get older, though may operate differently for boys and girls. For girls, the provision of emotional support and trust was clearly marked; this was less the case with the boys, but there were elements of this in some of the accounts from boys. Loyalty is important to children, and appears to be more-or-less taken for granted within families.

Symbolic relationships

For the children of Pakistani origin, religion is of central importance, and this came up in their descriptions of who is important as well as in group discussions in various ways. This is not surprising given the view from Muslim mothers that 'religion was the paramount influence in the way that they brought up their children' (Ali Shah, 1997, p. 14). Islam prescribes a set of moral principles and a way of life which is reflected in the children's definitions of family roles and relationships, and their accounts of who is important to them. For example:

> God is important to me because he made me and gave me life. (Shazia, 10)

> My mum is important to me because she . . . looks after me and she takes me to the mosque. (Nakila, 10)

> Who is important to me? Allah = God. Parents, Religions. God because there is no one except Allah, he made us. Parents = my parents brought me to this world. Religions – I follow my parents then I learn about religion. (Waqas, 13)

> My parents and my religion is important to me because my parents have took good care of me and give me birth. I have to follow my religion to be Muslim. (Saeed, 13)

In the group discussions, issues around religion frequently arose, for example, how many times a sister had read the Qur'ān and many of the children, both boys and girls, mentioned going to Mosque after school (indeed, they some-times referred to it as 'school') where they are taught the basic principles of Islam and to read and recite the Qur'ān (see Shaw, 1988; Dosanjh and Ghuman, 1996).

Only one Village child mentioned religion and Christianity, describing his church congregation as 'like a family'. This could reflect the way children constructed the question and they may have felt that it was not appropriate to mention religion in this context. The Young People's Social Attitudes survey of 580 12 to 19 year olds asked a direct question about religiosity and found that 62 per cent of 12 to 15 year olds said they do believe in God, and 12 per cent of 12 to 19 year olds attended a religious service once or more a week (Roberts, 1996). Islam provides a code for a way of life in quite a different way to Christianity and this was clear from these children's accounts. In particular, Islam puts great emphasis on the importance of family life and relationships between parents and children, and many verses of the Qur'ān and Ahādith elaborate on this (Hewitt, 1997).

Pets

When asked to draw or write about who is important, Village children all asked 'can we include our pets?', to which I responded 'yes'. This may have skewed subsequent responses as children then widened the range of 'who' they described. Pet animals (these included dogs, cats, mice, hamsters, guinea pigs, a goat, horses, African snails, parrots) were frequently drawn or mentioned by the Village children, markedly less so by the Town children, and it seems likely that pet ownership is more common in rural areas. However, for some children, pets are part of their families. Pets were not mentioned at all by the children of Pakistani origin.

Briefly, the reasons children gave for the importance of pets included the fact that they are 'funny', 'cuddly'; 'special', 'you can play with them, you can love them'; 'you can look after them' (many children mentioned proudly how long they had kept their pets alive way beyond their normal life expectancy); they are 'always your friends, they can't say anything back'; 'you trust them and they trust you'; 'in a way they're sort of part of your family, so you like respect 'em, love them'. One boy said, 'well, when they die, it's kind of like a family member dying, so you get all sad'. Pets represent a source of emotional comfort for some children, and this is frequently overlooked in accounts of children's social lives and rarely explored in any depth. Indeed, there may be a tendency to trivialise the relationship children have with their pets.

Summary and discussion

This section has discussed the significance to children of siblings, wider kin, friendships, religion and pets. The accounts of sibling and kin relationships show that for some children, brothers and/or sisters and wider kin are very meaningful. This is not differentiated by ethnic origin, though there may be differences in the obligations implicit in sibling relationships, in that siblings of Pakistani origin may be expected to play with and care for each other to a greater extent. Some children, regardless of ethnic background, described close and regular contact with their relatives, which they clearly value. For Muslim children, religion is extremely important as prescribing a way of life and set of moral principles, and has implications for how they view the concept 'family'. It is also likely to have implications for how they see themselves, their self-expression and expectations of 'being listened to', explored in the next section. Finally, pets obviously can be of central importance for some children, offering companionship to supplement that from family, kin and friends.

5. Listening to children

This section explores the children's discussions about 'being listened to' and 'having a say' in relation to family decision making. A broad range of topics, from the length of the working week, caning in schools, the state of school toilets to security measures in schools and violent intruders, were discussed. On the whole, the discussions about rights and participation were much fuller with the older children, though the data do show that younger children can engage meaningfully with notions of decision making and justice. Children also discussed what they knew about the UN Convention on the Rights of the Child, and whether they felt they had a say in making decisions (broadly speaking) in families, school and wider community, and whether they felt they were listened to. There was a possible cultural and/or linguistic difference for the youngest children of Pakistani origin, in that the notions of 'rights' and 'decisions' are complex ones, and I only explained them briefly (by talking about 'who decides, chooses' and 'what you can and can't have/do') if they did not appear to be familiar with the terms. The language of 'rights' in UN instruments is a western construction, and secular rather than religious (Henkin, 1990). Whether it can be transposed in a straightforward way to other cultures is not clear. In western culture, 'there is an emphasis on separateness, clear boundaries, individuality and autonomy within relationships' (Dwivedi, 1996, p. 160), while in eastern cultures, the person is embedded in sets of family relationships and the individual is not distinguished from their family, and rights are linked to roles, responsibilities and obligations. This is likely to have implications for how children see themselves and express themselves, given that they are taught to respect the authority of their elders (Henkin, 1990; Dosanjh and Ghuman, 1996).

When asked 'what do you think about being listened to, do you have a say in decisions?', many Village and older Town children responded by saying 'no, not really', though some disagreed and said 'I do' [get listened to]. On the whole the older children had much more to say about decision making in schools and the wider community, not discussed in this report. The youngest children of Pakistani origin tended to say that parents and other relatives made decisions for them, for example, 'My mum and my dad make all the decisions and my sisters'. Some mentioned themselves, 'Me and my mum decide'.

Ten-year-old boys of Pakistani origin saw the question about children's rights as being about physical punishment, though one boy did say about 'being listened to': 'Miss, when they talk we have to listen to them, when you talk, they listen to you'. In another group of boys the question led to a discussion about deciding who to marry, when to go to Mosque, whose choice it was and so on:

> Miss, in Islam, miss, when you get married, you don't have to listen to your parents, it's up to you, who you want to get married to . . . You want to go the Mosque, and your mum and dad say 'no don't go to the Mosque', it's your choice whether you wanna go or not . . .

> Another boy disagreed, saying 'no it's not, it's God's choice, you *have* to'.

> Researcher: So what about decisions, decisions are made for you, do you feel?
> Them: Yes . . . [unintelligible] sometimes we talk about if you're gonna do this or not . . . and they sometimes let you and sometimes don't . . . you discuss this . . .
> Boy: Children . . . sometimes their mum and dad don't let them make decisions, they make decisions for them . . . their children start hanging around with bad boys, then their mum and dad will lose their temper and start shouting, they're not gonna hit them or anything, just make the child *understand* . . .

Overall, the ten-year-old boys of Pakistani origin were much more voluble in discussions of decision making than the girls. Whether or not this reflects a cultural expectation to be obedient and honour elders, which may differ according to gender, is not clear, but girls may not be encouraged to speak out in the same way as boys (Dosanjh and Ghuman, 1996; Lau, 1988). The ten year old girls of Pakistani origin also described how parents and other adults make decisions on their behalf: 'I listen to my mum and dad, children should listen to parents, that's good manners'. Another girl added, 'You should respect your mum and dad'; and another, 'Miss, you should listen to your parents and love them'. Other girls mentioned mums, dads, brothers, sisters, and cousins, as making decisions.

In the older Village sample, one 12 year old boy said: 'If it's got something to do with children, I think they should have a say in it'. Another group of 12 year olds had the following discussion:

> Researcher: . . . what do you think about children's rights, being listened to, having a say in decision making . . .
>
> Megan: [interrupting] They don't! . . . well, they do sometimes, but mainly you're just told what to do, and with things at school, they ask the parents, but the parents aren't in the lessons . . . they just, if they just wanna ask you if you're not happy about things, they ask your parents, but parents don't go to the school so they won't know.
>
> Shannon: It's really unfair, because it's us that everything's based around, you know, we will be adults and be the world, so why shouldn't we have a say about what happens? It's like when you get new clothes, your mum says 'No, I hate that' but they don't have to wear it.

These girls are reflecting on the fact that frequently they are not directly 'listened to' and that parents may act as proxies to comment on their behalf. Further, gender is likely to have an important effect on which kinds of decisions children might be able to or allowed to take. A group of 14 year old girls commented:

> Researcher: Do you think you get listened to?
> Them: No . . . Not very much at school, but [we do] at home . . .
> Sophie: I think your parents care for you and they, like, listen to you.
> Stephanie: They wanna listen, in case you got a problem and it's serious, so they listen, in case it could involve getting hurt or something.
> Others: Yeah!

Stacey: 'Cos they would listen because they care for you
               more than the people at school do . . . 'cos they're
               your flesh and blood, in't yer . . .
Sophie: . . . and teachers probably have problems of their
               own at home . . .

In another group, Melanie, 13, said 'it depends. If you've got
a good point to say, then they listen, but if you haven't, they
just shut off. Oh, it's only a kid, you know.' In a different
group, a 13 year old boy said: 'children's opinions should
count, because if you did it all on adult's opinions it wouldn't
be fair for the children'. Another boy in the same group said
'most people listen to adults instead of children'. Some
children commented on how they felt that they had not had
enough of a say in specific family matters. One group of 12
year olds had the following discussion:

> Callum: I think it's very important because sometimes you're
> supposed to be making family decisions, and the children just
> pushed out of it, it's just the parents making the decisions . . .
>
> John: I have that going on at the moment, with my mum and
> dad, they're deciding who, when I'm gonna see my dad and
> when I'm gonna see my mum, and then not concerning me
> when I want to do anything. Like I had this football
> tournament going on in Canada, and my dad wanted me for
> that week to take me to France, somewhere, and I wanna go to
> football, but mum's arguing that she wants me to stay home,
> my dad's arguing that he wants me to go to France with him,
> and I'm not getting a decision in anything at the moment [all of
> this said quite lightly and matter-of-factly].
>
> Researcher: Yeah, it's difficult, isn't it?
>
> John: Yeah . . .
>
> Callum: If it's got something to do with children, I think they
> should have a say in it.

From their point of view, these children appear to want to
have a say in decisions rather than make the decisions
themselves. Some were clearer about this, as in the following
extract from a discussion with a group of nine year old Village
children:

> Sam (a boy): I think mums and dads should listen to children
> so children can get what they want when they want, go where
> they want, all the time, and they never have to do what their
> mums and dads have to do.

Keri: [that's] not fair, what about the grown-ups? . . . When you grow up, you want to do what you want, when you want, get what you want, and it's not gonna be like that, you've got to do what your children say, you've had this all your life, and your children are going to feel like left out, you're going to be taking care of yourself all the time, when you want, going where you want, [interrupted] . . . you'd get selfish, and you wouldn't have any respect for any other people, you'd just have respect for yourself and nobody else.

Other children interjected but she continued 'but we can't always get our own way, we should get our own way sometimes, but not all the time . . .'.

In a discussion with Village 11 year olds, Nicole disagreed with her classmates and said 'No, I don't think they should get what they want, most of the time . . . they've got to have something over you, you know, haven't they; you can't just go wandering off and doing exactly what you want'. This view was expanded on in a different group, of 14 year old girls:

Stacey: It depends how old you are, whether you make all your decisions or not, when you get old enough to make important decisions for your future, and that sort of thing, I think you should be given help in making decisions . . .

Charlotte: . . . my mum thinks I'm old enough to make decisions . . . but I don't feel that I am ready to make all the decisions yet in my family, but I can make some, like what I was gonna do, or something, but I haven't made hardly any decisions, important ones, recently.

Sophie: I think like your mum and dad like try and push you to make your own decisions . . . I think some decisions you should make for yourself . . . but sometimes there are some decisions that you can't make on your own, you need to like either get your friends involved, or your teachers or your parents, or your family . . .

These accounts suggest that making decisions is not straightforward. The girls in the above extract recognise that as they get older, children need to make more decisions, but that they need to have some help in doing so. They express an awareness of the limits of their capacity to be independent, and are clear that the decision-making process depends on what the decision is about and who it involves.

Summary and discussion

This section has shown a range of responses to the question about being listened to and having a say in decisions. Some children did feel they had a say in family decision-making, others did not. Most children felt it was important to have a say in matters affecting them, though this varied according to gender and ethnicity. This may be an area which merits further research. However, quite young children could engage meaningfully with the notion of rights and being listened to. Some of the children seemed to reflect that they would like to have a say in the process of decision making, to be heard, not that they make decisions on their own or have ultimate control over the decision-making process. They want to be talked to and consulted, and given information, and to be able to give their point of view and have their opinions taken into account. Even quite young children saw decision making as potentially problematic and could see this from others' perspectives.

6. Conclusions

There are a number of conclusions to be drawn from this research. This project set out to explore how some children define the concept of 'family', with the intention of providing points of reference and contextual information for practitioners and professionals working with children where children's views and opinions need to be elicited. Whether or not these findings can be generalised to wider samples of children could be usefully explored in further research.

When children were asked about what they thought counted as 'family' in terms of structure, younger children in particular tended to see children, marriage and physical presence as being the key constituents of 'a family'. This was particularly marked among the children of Pakistani origin and reflects cultural norms and kinship patterns. However, when discussing these questions in groups, some children were clear that parents, or more precisely, fathers, can be absent for all sorts of reasons; they can be divorced, dead, away on business, or working abroad. Physical absence does not necessarily signify emotional absence, though for some children the presence of a father was necessary to define family.

In their own definitions of what a family is, and what families are for, children presented a more complicated picture, in which love, care, mutual respect and support rather than structure (such as marriage and the presence of children) were the key characteristics. This was the case regardless of gender, ethnicity, and age, though children's definitions were more detailed the older they were. Further, some older children expressed a view that 'happiness' in family life cannot be taken for granted.

The centrality to children of parents, especially mothers, as providers of physical and emotional support, was also clear.

For younger children in particular, parents' roles were described as being clearly differentiated according to gender. Girls saw their mothers as important as someone to talk to, while boys were less likely to describe the need to have someone to talk to.

Sibling relationships were also important, and while these relationships often involve fighting and rivalry, children often described their siblings very affectionately. Further, some brothers and sisters clearly provide a good deal of support to each other. For the older children in the sample, friendships were important to them. Girls described their close friends as central for emotional support, though there were elements of this in a few of the accounts from boys. Some children described family members as 'friends' and other children described friends as like 'mothers', or 'brothers and sisters', suggesting that kin terms can be interchangeable and can describe the closeness of the relationship.

Further, for some children, social life appeared to revolve around wider kin, and this appeared to be the case regardless of ethnic background.

Pets were an important source of companionship and comfort for some children, particularly the younger children in the Village sample.

The differences between the groups of children were that some children of Pakistani origin described large nuclear families and close relationships with their siblings. They were also likely to see a father's absence as being related to work or travel rather than divorce. Their religious beliefs were very important to them, and this is reflected in how they answered specific questions in the research.

There were some differences in the way younger and older children defined family and described who was important to them. Younger children seemed to present fairly concrete explanations. For example, they focused on provision, particularly in their discussions of who is important. They tended not to draw on abstract representations of relationships, and were likely to draw on their own situations and experiences to explore these issues. Older children were more generalised in their use of language and did draw on abstract notions.

Narrow definitions of 'the family' as 'nuclear' are ethnocentric and obscure a wide diversity in family forms and family practices. Children appeared to have an accepting, inclusive view of what counts as family and their definitions did not centre around the 'nuclear norm' or biological relatedness. Children's households appeared to provide a supportive setting and these households could encompass a range of significant others, including pets. In other words, the people who matter to children are the people who are available to them and around them.

When it came to decision making, children in the study seemed to be asking to be able to 'have a say' in what happens to them, rather than be asking to make decisions themselves. There is a difference between being asked to decide, and feeling that you are being consulted and listened to and provided with information. Some children did feel they are listened to within their families, others did not, and others expressed a feeling that 'decision making' is not straightforward, and that they do not necessarily want to be burdened with it.

Implications for policy and practice

There are a number of implications arising from this research. Firstly, the report has described a progression from children's responses to closed questions (requiring yes/no answers) of what counted as family for children, to their responses to open-ended questions and discussions of definitions of family, and who is important to them. There was a corresponding progression in the children's ideas, in that when the closed questions were discussed in groups, responses were much more varied, intricate and qualified. This may have implications for how we talk to children about family life, in other words, relying on closed questions which require yes/no answers may be too narrow, and a range of different techniques and ways of exploring children's views may be more constructive.

Secondly, the finding that some children, regardless of ethnic background, described having a great deal of regular contact with wider kin, is in contrast to assumptions about the declining importance of family relationships. It also contrasts with ethnocentric social policy and legal conceptualisations of 'the family' as nuclear, though the fact that grandparents' rights to see their grandchildren have been acknowledged in the Children Act 1989 (Section 8) is a step in recognising that 'families' are more than nuclear.

Thirdly, the research also raised questions about the application of concepts such as rights and self-expression to cultures and religions where notions of self and appropriate expressions of emotion may be different to those of the dominant culture. In other words, there may be implications for issues relating to children's rights and participation in decision making in contexts where respect for parents or elders is paramount.

Fourthly, social policy conceptualisations of childhood tend to depict children as a unitary, homogenous category. In practice, children have a wide range of characteristics, experiences and backgrounds. Children of different ages described 'family' in different ways and the report noted that younger children used concrete examples and their own experiences in discussions, while older children were more abstract. However, there was wide variation between children of whatever age, and some eight and nine year olds showed a clear capacity to step outside their own circumstances to generalise, and to see things from others' points of view.

Fifthly, children's reflections on participation and 'being listened to', in which they were clear that they should 'have a say' in decisions about them, has implications for ascertaining children's opinions in custody, care and post-separation cases and other circumstances in which decisions are made on behalf of children. Following the Children Act 1989, the focus has been on asking children of divorcing parents where they want to live, but a corresponding fear of overburdening children with the responsibility for making this decision may arise. However, consultation with children could be broadened out to include other areas and levels of participation in decision making, but this needs to be sensitive to cultural and religious contexts. Further, when decisions about their care are being made it is clear that the wider contexts of children's social relationships, including their extended family, friendships and even pets, need to be taken into account. The fact that pets are important to young children is often noted by researchers but rarely explored in any depth, possibly because it is seen as trivial and essentially childish. This in turn may enable adults to trivialise other expressed wishes or views from children.

Finally, debates about the effects on children of family breakdown and reconstitution have generated an image of children as passive and vulnerable. There is an inherent tension between protecting children from the harmful effects of family conflict, and enabling children to be active participants in decisions about their welfare. This study has shown that children can be resourceful, constructive commentators. The challenge now is how to enable adults to listen to children's opinions and integrate these views into decision making at a range of levels.

References

Afshar, H (1995) 'Muslim women in West Yorkshire: growing up with real and imaginary values amidst conflicting views of self and society' *in* Afshar, H and Maynard, M *eds The Dynamics of 'race' and gender: some feminist interventions.* Routledge

Ahmad, W I U (1996) 'Family obligations and social change among Asian communities' *in* Ahmad, W I U and Atkin, K *eds 'Race' and Community Care.* Open University Press

Alderson, P (1995) *Listening to Children. Children, Ethics and Social Research.* Barnardos

Ali Shah, T (1997) 'Parenting and Asian families', *The Parenting Forum Newsletter,* 8. National Children's Bureau

Bernardes, J (1997) *Family Studies: An Introduction.* Routledge

Berndt, T J and Ladd, G W *eds* (1989) *Peer relationships in child development.* New York/Chichester: Wiley

Brannen, J *ed.* (1992) *Mixing Methods: Qualitative and Quantitative Research.* Avebury

Butler, I and Williamson, H (1994) *Children speak. Children, trauma and social work.* NSPCC/Longman

Central Statistical Office (CSO) (1994) *Social focus on children.* HMSO

Clarke, K, Craig, G and Glendinning, C (1996) *Children's views on child support: parents, families and responsibilities.* The Children's Society

Dosanjh, J S and Ghuman, P A S (1996) *Child-rearing in ethnic minorities.* Multilingual Matters

Duncombe, J and Marsden, D (1993) 'Love and intimacy: the gender division of emotion and "emotion work"', *Sociology,* 27, 2, 221–41

Dunn, J (1993) *Young children's close relationships. Beyond attachment.* Sage

Dwivedi, K N (1996) 'Race and the child's perspective' *in* Davie, R, Upton, G and Varma, V *eds The voice of the child: a handbook for professionals.* Falmer Press

Ennew, J (1994) Childhood as a social phenomenon. National Report, England and Wales. Eurosocial Report 36/16, European Centre, Vienna

Ennew, J and Milne, B (1989) *The next generation. Lives of Third World children.* Zed Books

Finch, J and Mason, J (1993) *Negotiating family responsibilities.* Routledge

Gilby, R L and Pederson, D R (1982) 'The development of the child's concept of the family', *Canadian Journal of Behavioural Science*, 14, 2, 110–21

Griffiths, V (1995) *Adolescent girls and their friends: feminist ethnography.* Avebury

Gubrium, J F and Holstein, J A (1990) *What is family?* Mountain View, California: Mayfield Publishing Co

Henkin, L (1990) *The age of rights.* New York: Columbia University Press

Hewitt, I B (1997) *What does Islam say?* The Muslim Educational Trust

Hey, V (1997) *The company she keeps: an ethnography of girls' friendships.* Open University Press

Hill, M and Tisdall, K (1997) *Children and society.* Longman

Holland, P (1992) *What is a Child? Popular Images of Childhood.* Virago

Hylton, C (1995) *Coping with change. Family transitions in multi-cultural communities.* National Stepfamily Association

James, A (1995) 'Methodologies of competence for a competent methodology?' Paper presented to Children and Social Competence Conference, Guildford, Surrey, July 1995

James, A (1996) 'Learning to be friends', *Childhood*, 3, 3, 313–30

James, A and Prout, A eds (1990) *Constructing and Reconstructing Childhood.* Falmer Press

Jenks, J (1996) *Childhood.* Routledge.

Lansdown, G (1994) 'Children's rights' *in* Mayall, B ed. *Children's childhoods. Observed and experienced.* Falmer Press

Lansdown, G (1995) *Taking Part: Children's participation in decision making.* Institute for Public Policy Research

Lau, A (1988) 'Family therapy and ethnic minorities' *in* Street, E and Dryden, W eds *Family Therapy in Britain.* Open University Press

Lucchini, R (1996) 'Theory, method and triangulation in the study of children', *Childhood: A Global Journal of Child Research*, 3, 2, 167–70

McGlone, F, Park, A and Roberts, C (1996/7) 'Relative values: kinship and friendship' *in* Jowell, R and others eds *British Social Attitudes: the 13th Report.* Gower

Makrinioti, D (1994) 'Conceptualisation of childhood in a welfare state: a critical reappraisal' *in* Qvortrup, J and others eds *Childhood matters. Social theory, practice and politics.* Avebury

Mitchell, A (1985) *Children in the middle: living through divorce.* Tavistock

Modood, T, Beishon, S and Virdee, S (1994) *Changing ethnic identities.* Policy Studies Institute

Moore, M, Sixsmith, J and Knowles, K (1996) *Children's reflections on family life.* Falmer Press

Morgan, D (1996) *Family connections: an introduction to family studies.* Polity Press

Morrow, V (1997) 'Methods, ethics and children: preliminary thoughts from a research project on children's definitions of family'. Paper presented to Urban Childhood Conference, Trondheim, Norway, June 1997

Morrow, V (1998) '"If you were a teacher, it would be harder to talk to you": reflections on qualitative research with children in schools'. Draft paper submitted to the *International Journal of Social Research Methodology*

Morrow, V (forthcoming) '"It's cool, 'cos you can't give us detentions and things, can you?!": reflections on research with children' *in* Milner, P and Carolin, B *Listening to children: a handbook for practitioners*. Routledge

Morrow, V and Richards, M P M (1996) 'The ethics of social research with children: an overview', *Children & Society*, 10, 90–105

O'Brien, M and Jones, D (1997) 'The absence and presence of fathers: accounts from children's diaries' *in* Bjornberg, U and Kollind, A-K *eds Men's family relations*. Goteborg: University of Goteborg Publications

O'Brien, M, Alldred, P and Jones, D (1996) 'Children's constructions of family and kinship' *in* Brannen, J and O'Brien, M *eds Children in families. Research and policy*. Falmer Press

Ribbens, J (1994) *Mothers and their Children: a feminist sociology of childrearing*. Sage

Roberts, H (1996) '"It wasn't like this in our day": young people, religion and right and wrong' *in* Roberts, H and Sachdev, D *eds Having Their Say – The views of 12–19 year olds*. Barnardos

Roberts, H and Sachdev, D *eds* (1996) *Having Their Say – The views of 12–19 year olds*. Barnardos

Robertson Elliot, F (1996) *Gender, family and society*. Macmillan

Roffey, S, Tarrant, T and Majors, K (1994) *Young friends: schools and friendship*. Cassell

Rubin, Z (1981) *Children's friendships*. Fontana

Saifullah Khan, V (1979) *Minority Families in Britain: Support and Stress*. Macmillan

Scott, J (1997) 'Changing households in Britain: do families still matter?', *The Sociological Review*, 45, 4, 591–620

Shaw, A (1988) *A Pakistani community in Britain*. Blackwell

Skolnick, A (1991) *Embattled Paradise: The American Family in the Age of Uncertainty*. New York: Basic Books

Walczak, Y and Burns, S (1984) *Divorce: the child's point of view*. Harper & Row

Index